Perceptions

Gillian Bickley

Proverse Hong Kong

Perceptions

PERCEPTIONS consists of short pieces, poetry or poem-like essays, written over a period of thirty years, on various serious and reflective topics, but with some humorous and occasional work too. As in Gillian Bickley's previous collections, the subjects occur internationally: this time, in the Pyrenees, Nigeria, Hawai'i, Albania, as well as Hong Kong. Taken as a whole, this fifth poetry collection recognizes the need for shelter and survival, the desire for love, for achievement, for feelings of self-worth, for objects on which to bestow reciprocal affection and the search for high-order achievements beyond the self. Reaching beyond this, *Perceptions* considers the needs of other species, our responsibilities towards them and the fragile environment that we all share.

GILLIAN BICKLEY was born and educated in the United Kingdom, and has lived mostly in Hong Kong since 1970. Her books include *China Suite and other Poems* (2009), *Sightings: a collection of Poetry* (2007), *Moving House and other Poems from Hong Kong* (2005) and *For the Record and other Poems of Hong Kong* (2003) The latter two are now also published in Chinese translations. She is the author of *The Stewarts of Bourtreebush* (2003) and *The Golden Needle: The Biography of Frederick Stewart (1836-1889)* (1997), and editor of *The Complete Court Cases of Magistrate Frederick Stewart* (2008), *A Magistrate's Court in Nineteenth Century Hong Kong: Court in Time* (2005; 2nd edition, 2009), *The Development of Education in Hong Kong, 1841-1897* (2002) and *Hong Kong Invaded! A '97 Nightmare* (2001). Her poetry has been anthologised in Hong Kong, the Philippines and the United Kingdom & translated into several languages.

Supported by

The Hong Kong Arts Development Council fully supports freedom of artistic expression. The views and opinions expressed in this project do not represent the stand of the Council.

Perceptions

Gillian Bickley

Proverse Hong Kong

Perceptions
by Gillian Bickley.
2nd edition published in pbk (no CD) in Hong Kong
by Proverse Hong Kong, December 2016.
Copyright © Gillian Bickley, December 2016.
ISBN:978-988-8228-56-0
Available from: https://createspace.com/6650796

1st published in pbk in Hong Kong by Proverse Hong Kong
(packaged with an audio recording on CD
of all poems in the collection read by the author)
23 March 2012.
Copyright © Gillian Bickley, 23 March 2012.
ISBN 978-988-19934-5-8

Distribution and other enquiries:
Proverse Hong Kong, P. O. Box 259, Tung Chung Post Office,
Tung Chung, Lantau Island, NT, Hong Kong SAR, China.
E-mail: proverse@netvigator.com
Web site: www.proversepublishing.com

The right of Gillian Bickley to be identified as the author of this work
has been asserted by her
in accordance with the Copyright, Designs and Patents Act 1988.

Cover photograph by and © Proverse Hong Kong.
Cover design by Artist Hong Kong Company.
Page design by Proverse Hong Kong.

All rights reserved. No part of this publication may be reproduced, stored in a retrieval system, or transmitted, in any form or by any means, electronic, mechanical, photocopying, recording or otherwise, without the prior written permission of the publisher or publisher and author. The book is sold subject to the condition that it shall not, by way of trade or otherwise, be lent, re-sold, hired out or otherwise circulated without the author's prior written consent in any form of binding or cover other than that in which it is published and without a similar condition including this condition being imposed on the subsequent owner or purchaser. Please contact Proverse Hong Kong (acting as agent for the author) in writing, to request any and all permissions (including but not restricted to republishing, inclusion in anthologies, translation, reading, performance and use as set pieces in examinations and festivals).

British Library Cataloguing in Publication Data
A catalogue record for the first edition of this book
is available from the British Library.

Perceptions

Dedicated to my husband, Verner Bickley, patient, energetic, supportive, understanding, creative...

Perceptions

Preface

The poems making up Gillian Bickley's *Perceptions* possess a certain delicacy of arrangement—a panoply, an array of pieces, placed before us to examine one by one. We feel the heft of each in our hand, replace it, and then move to the next. We read on, realizing with wonder that her poems, too, are energetic and motile. They respond to our touch, assume sentience and, sometimes, take flight.

When looking back at the on-going development of Bickley's career as a poet, we may perceive the laudable emergence of restraint. Many of the poems collected in *Perceptions* verge on sentiment, peering at it, sometimes wanting it, and then step decisively back. It is such proximity to sentiment, without the eventual indulgence in emotion or nostalgia, which makes Bickley's poems winning, as in the bold truth declared in the long poem, 'Added Value', that opens the volume:

> a continuing lesson
> that this world's goods fail us and die.

So do we, Bickley's readers, recognize ourselves (failing and dying) in these lines, so many pure products gone crazy in a clear echo of William Carlos Williams. The title, 'Added Value', recalls the modern and diminished sense of human intercourse (which, most delightfully, once referred to everything apart from sex) now reduced to a trite neologism used in commerce and trade. Bickley laments such loss of meaningful connection among persons, and the cheapness of fashionable substitutes for it. And so should we.

There is similar courage and an invitation to faith in 'The Aim of Life', the message of which is to "develop our souls"—a familiar enough refrain, if the call didn't sustain such pertinence and cogency here, in Hong Kong, where soulfulness ranks only slightly higher than yesterday's tickertape. In defiance of the material and exclusive, Bickley has added real spiritual value on behalf of those who endeavor to craft English words in the unique setting that only a home in Hong Kong can provide. English has to be fought for a little bit harder these days, but Bickley's press and publications show no strain. She has sustained over the years a long and broad affection for this Chinese place, with an unshakable sensibility expressed in a language whose properties she cherishes and, most probably, cannot live without. Even more important, Gillian Bickley would not and cannot do without English here.

It is prophesied by the pundits, in cries echoing along the halls of our academies, that the poetry of postcolonial Hong Kong may well be written in English, but not necessarily any longer by the English whose best times are merely retrograde in the imagining. Blinded as we are by the present dispensation—whatever is, we are told, is right—this may well be. But still the living set pieces inhabiting Bickley's imagination persist. The poignance of her many perceptions crowds upon us, and her poems gaze back with the Blakean fixity of a tiger. (As in 'Cats', where the poet has stared down the tiger of an unknown future and survived.)

This unblinking poise is Bickley's monument to the thriving literature of anglophone Hong Kong poetry in the present and future tenses: to persist, to witness, to testify. To remain.

Stuart Christie

Author's Introduction

Perceptions consists of short pieces, poetry or poem-like essays, written over a period of thirty years, on various serious and reflective topics, with sections entitled, "Issues and Intimacies", "One Species", "Staring", "Passing On", "Reading On and In", "Times and Occasions", "Meetings and Memories".

The subject-matter of "Issues and Intimacies" includes a suggested argument by which God can be put back in the centre of human admiration, argues the need for changes in attitudes one culture towards another, describes the impact of technology on the centuries'-long predominance of the humanities, questions certain academic viewpoints relating to translation and also to reading theory and suggests that visiting writers need to listen to those they visit, at the same time as they ask for a hearing themselves.

"One Species" seeks to understand the world from the point of view of caged and domestic creatures, and argues that our concern to preserve animal species would also develop conditions more favourable than at present to the survival of the human race.

"Staring" contains a group of poems on subjects which clearly bear what has come to be seen as my signature: people seen in the street, or at a social distance, the privileged and the disadvantaged, leaders and the led, the solitary and the grouped, with reflections on their thoughts, feelings, lives, how others see them, the changes that habitat development will force upon them.

"Passing On" responds to the loss of two individuals.

"Reading On and In" consists of *jeux d'esprit* arising, on the one hand, from misreading of words and sights and, on the other hand, miscommunication through words and images.

Perceptions

"Times and Occasions" includes some humorous occasional poems as well as a plangent record of one special moment in time. "Meetings and Memories" is mainly composed of recent experiences, mostly in Hong Kong; descriptions, responses, interpretations, lessons; and one novelty poem produced following a writing workshop and finding its meaning only after a title emerged some weeks after composition.

The occasions that gave rise to the reflections and perceptions recorded here vary between a visit to a Hong Kong flower-show, attendance at a concert of medieval instruments in a remote Catalan village in the Pyrenees, walking down a road in down-town Lagos, Nigeria, visiting a museum in Honolulu, Hawai'i, visiting the museum of ethnography at Kruje Castle, Albania and early morning perambulation in a pleasant park in Discovery Bay, Lantau Island.

The collection as a whole recognizes the need for shelter and survival, the desire for love, for achievement, for feelings of self-worth, for objects on which to bestow reciprocal affection and the search for high-order achievements beyond the self. Unintentionally, the collection embodies an expression of Maslow's "Hierarchy of Needs".

Publication Acknowledgements
'"In a Handbag?!"' and 'Embodiment' were first published under the title, "Bags and Bagpipers" in IMPRINT, Issue 9, Hong Kong, WiPS, 2010, pp. 83-84. 'I touched the Wall' was first published in IMPRINT, Issue 10, Hong Kong, Women in Publishing Society, 2011, pp. 76-77. 'An almost human voice' and 'Intimates' will appear in IMPRINT, Issue 11, Women in Publishing Society, 2012.

'Choices' was first published under the title, 'Geoffrey Bonsall, RIP' in the Memorial booklet created by Geoffrey Emerson.

Table of Contents

Preface by Stuart Christie   7
Author's Introduction   9

ISSUES AND INTIMACIES
Added Value   14
Change Please!   18
The Aim of Life   21
International Intimacies   25
Language Learning   27
True Translation   28
Papal Visit   30
Passengers   32
International Relations   33

ONE SPECIES
Cats   36
Variety   40
An Almost Human Voice   43
Intimates   44

STARING
Don't Stare!   48
Lion's Pride   49
Cross-culturally-clothed   50
"In a handbag?!"   50
Free Daily Newspaper   51
Flower Show, 2009   52
Aesthetic Taste   53
Embodiment   54
The Blessed Ones   55
Kindness   56
"An Action Produces an Equal and Equivalent Reaction"?   58
Yoked   59
Widespread   59
Legs   60

Perceptions

Construction, Destruction   61
PASSING ON
Storage Space   64
Choices   65
READING ON AND IN
Dangerous Mis-Communication   68
Truer Than it Seems   68
Eden Marriage Registry   69
Suspension Cables   70
Persuasion   71
TIMES AND OCCASIONS
Eve of New Year's Eve   74
Middle Age   74
Christmas Party   75
Writers' Party   76
Penguin Party   76
Lessons from the Plants, 1   77
Lessons from the Plants, 2   77
MEETINGS AND MEMORIES
Friends   80
Daylight   81
Memory   82
I Touched the Wall   83
Pride   86
On Bus Number Eleven   86
Water   87
Individualist / Social Critic   88
The Senses of Morning   89

Notes   93

Perceptions

Issues and Intimacies

Added Value

The paradoxes in what we were taught!

Injunctions to store up treasure in heaven,
where neither rust nor moth would destroy,
were surely meant to teach us priorities;
Not, to eschew possessions.
Not, to neglect their care and repair.

Inbuilt obsolescence
would otherwise
be just what the Bible ordered—
a continuing lesson
that this world's goods fail us and die.

Advertising even
(in some strange way its twin),
does not hope to make us
covet cars, cookers, or clothes
for themselves,
but for the possibilities
they may facilitate
for spiritual solace, emotional joy.

Does the man exist who values objects for themselves
alone?

That extreme of spiritual poverty—
the miserable miser—
whose love of money
has lost sight
of its power to purchase,
presumably loves its power to move his heart?

Perceptions

The mother who wounds her children's hearts—
shields books, pictures and glass,
carved wood and carpets
from their desire to play—
values the work (the time,
the skill, the patience)
of those who made them;
those who developed technologies,
over variables of time;
those who thought the thoughts
that developing skills
have expressed.

She cherishes her own work also:—
the controlled and complicated
easy simplicity which
she has made a home.

No wonder, the strength of the work ethic!—
the pealing response rung
by the added value of Marx!—
since it seems we
naturally
see value
in everything tangible;

either serving the needs of our souls,
or embodying work and creativeness.

Quite naturally, then,
we would value nature and ourselves—
all things that are—
the more, if we thought of them like this:
created by a technologist
of massive range and intellect,
a visionary

Perceptions

with immense power of synthesis,

a being
who took pleasure in the creations of His hands,

expanding His humanity
by their existence,

the possibilities they give
for further work and love.

Should we not
try to embrace this concept? ...
extrapolate from our experience of man's works
(what he can do, has done, may do);
from our knowledge of man's
many conscious intentions,
seen even in fields and woods,
flowers and breeds of dogs,
milk-yield in cows,
cloud-seeded rainfall,
and babies in test-tubes?

Could we not extrapolate?
... accept
the possibility
that conscious intention
made the world and us?

And then—as artifacts—
might we value ourselves the more—
the others we know, the millions we know not,
the beasts and the forests, water and air?—
And if we estimate
the added value
of aeons of labour and vision,
the technological

Perceptions

inventiveness
and complexity
that made us and the world,

would we not be convinced,
in our own terms,
of what we should value most?

and restore our thoughts, ourselves,
and all things in our power,

to ordered harmony?

1982

Perceptions

Change Please!

The need for change perceived during a visit to the United States of America.

Is it because I've lived too long
in foreign parts,
that I feel it shocking to find
men of European stock in menial jobs,
waiting at tables,
punching tickets on trains?

At first I thought it was.

I've lived so long in places
where they work only
in the professions,
with spectacles, books and suits;
and where their wives (who would quite like
to work in shops, in hairdressers',
or hospitals) can't,
because of social pressure
—the same which, in 18th century India
and the 19th century too,
made the English combine
to pay the passage home
of any lesser white—jockey or failed businessman—
who let the side down,
creating (as they felt then) an Achille's heel
in the foot of the mighty Raj—

but there were other reasons too (language problems,
the need for jobs by the locals,
who lacked expatriate perks).

My assumption had grown to be

Perceptions

that such persons are educated.
So, I think, "What a waste of education
for this man to punch holes in tickets all day long,
telling us, 'Next stop, White Plains:
Change here for local trains!
This train will make White Plains,
One Twenty-Fifth street—One Twenty-Five—
and Grand Central only!'"

But now I know my feeling is
more valuable
than I at first supposed.

In a culture, whose goals are
spiritual unity with the universe,
love of beauty, children, man and woman;

collecting tickets implies no failure;
is irrelevant to the goals of life.

But when career-achievement is the culture's goal,
how lacking, what failures menials are!

Pity the European!

Unless we change his culture,
it is likely that, to save his soul,
he will still want others to be his menials;

and they will accept, because it does not matter
to them to labour.

Their humiliation exists
only in the eyes of some persons from Europe,
whose eyes see them, coloured
by differently-thinking thoughts.

Perceptions

This produces,
most unfortunately,
situations which
make it difficult
for the European to know
his own culture's failings.

How can a culture lived by men—
failures
in his culture's eyes—
be more complete than his,
occupied by successful men in suits?

We need a prophet. Things must change.
But how?

1982, Revised 2006

The Aim of Life

"The aim of life is to develop our souls:

"Like the Wanderer,
that Anglo-Saxon pilgrim,
who saw his journey through life
as a struggle to return to a heaven,
that had inexplicably
banished him;
sent him out from the warm fireside,
where men huddle
against the monsters
and inhospitable nature;
secure in the companionship of man,
secure under the patronage
of the warring and feudal lord;

"Like Wordsworth's child,
born in the presence of God's glory—
his vision of eternity
dulled by living in the world;
bitterly regretting
the distance from God
that life brings,
and fighting
to live in such a way
as to regain God's bright presence
after death."

So we were taught in school.

Religion, philosophy, morality,
the world's literatures—
these were central to our studies;
for they showed us the way to live,

Perceptions

to secure safe passage to heaven at death;
the trumpets' sound for us on the other side.

Science ... technology ...
were merely means
to illustrate God's almightiness ...
spreading our knowledge of him.

By reducing the toil of life,
they left more time to study Him.

But now Society has forgotten God,
no longer views as actual
immortality of the individual
(for man may soon destroy
the whole human race for ever) ....

Now come to this pass, what part
can humanities play?

Technology is all-important.
It can kill us. It can starve us. It can feed us.
It can do almost all that God could do.

Soon it will do anything.

In this world,
only technology
seems relevant.

All the humanities can do
is teach us how to live
in a technological world;
how to adjust our values
and desires
to cope.

A whole study,
whose very ethos
teaches its own primacy,
is forced into irrelevance …
subordination to a knowledge
it must believe is secondary.

No wonder we—
trained in the humanities—
are sad, suicidal, frustrated,
aggressive and depressed.

Should we fight against
the general current of things?
Or—more difficult—
against our common sense?
… insisting
— but how argue this? —
on the centrality
of our own pursuits and skills?

Or, should we accept
that we, who chose the humanities,
because of our desire to work
on the most important,
are now firmly lodged
in work which is peripheral;
and have no hope
—at this time of our lives—
to gain sufficient expertise
in the study of the new gods
… of technology…
and the morality they insist on:

(cruel gods who require our sacrifice
of loyalty, unselfishness,
endurance and love

Perceptions

—qualities centuries have nurtured—
our sacrifice, also, of
our previous choice
of future good
over present gratification;
the distant not the immediate goal).

It cannot be that we
must bend our skills,
our love of whatsoever things are true,
whatsoever things are pure,
whatsoever things are good and of good report;
our search to make man worthy of God's love
and man's eternal destiny, given by God.

It cannot be, that we
must strive, now,
to help man live this life
alone;
and in harmony
only
with machines,
that man has made.

International Intimacies

We meet. We part.
In between
we make acquaintance, become friends,
understand how much we have in common,
how we complement each other;
see what we could do together
if we did not live
across the world….

across cultures too.

But these aren't the problem.

These we transcend easily,
finding common ground:—
music, cultures we admire,
causes we support,
experiences, ideas,
global news we share,
compassionate objects
that have moved us
equally.

We teeter on the edges
of such deep intimacy
that we withdraw;
experience the empty feelings
of incipient depression.

Is it too much to cherish?—
this sudden intimacy of the shared cause,
that our international meetings focused on,
and which we can—no, will—pursue.
But we have other lives.

Perceptions

We return to them. These relationships
descend deep within our daily consciousness.

Some of us will treasure them;
restore them, when we meet again.

Some will be angry or disappointed,
that constant communication
did not continually vibrate across the wires.

The seeds fell on the deepest ground,
began to sprout bright green;

but the field was already occupied.

2009

Language Learning

Learning another language is a useful task.
You can act as interpreter;
explain what others ask,
pass on the replies.

Learning another language is a useful step
for learning about language.

Seeing how languages differ,
we grasp how languages work,
see language as a system.

And culture too.

We see culture creating language,
and language enshrining culture.

Translation and interpretation
are interesting tasks.
Learning about cultures
and the nature and system of language
is interesting too.

But, other than this,
learning languages is pretty dull;
learning other ways of saying just the same thing;
making the medium, it seems,
more weighty than the message.

As for me, I'd rather spend my time
finding more things to say.
Andorra, 2006

Perceptions

True Translation

Where some succeed in exact and difficult tasks,
others can only seek to succeed or follow the fad.

When they fail,
or lack the character
to persevere to success,
a new fashion is declared.
"We can do it differently.
Perfection is not necessary. Imperfection
is more free, creative; better ... yes,
better!" they assert.

Translation is one example.
Reading is another.

All sorts of theories have come up
from the surely inaccurate premise,
that it is not necessary to seek to grasp
the author's meaning.
"He had no meaning," some say. "He didn't
Write the words. The words wrote him."

As for translation,
"It is a creative act of its own," some say,
and I agree.
"The product is a new creative work."
I agree again.
But isn't the creative act a different kind?

Should not translators first understand a work,
then render the same faithfully,
in a way they consider best communicates
the original meaning in another language?
... and to its readers in the target language?

If this is not what they do, or plan to do,
should not the translator
first pay me
for using my work
as a springboard
for his own?

... and not me, him,
for <u>not</u> translating my work?

Not reading and not translating are all very well,
if you can't manage to read, can't manage to translate.

But it is the real readers and translators,
the Marie and Pierre Curies of the literary world,
whose self-denial, selfless submission
to the meanings of others
will eventually save us all!

Andorra, 2006

Perceptions

Papal Visit

"I begin with the words of Saint Augustine,
'Pox [*sic* 'pox'] deum', 'The Peace of God'"—
so the interpreter renders it
(a freudian slip if there ever was!);
but what was really said, surely, was,
"Pax vobiscum", "Peace be with you!"

Calm face;
but quick shallow breathing
shows the nervousness
beneath worried eyes,
as a black American
sings The Lord's Prayer.

Who wanted that large inset BBC face
wittering on about sex abuse,
forcing Il Papa out of centre screen?—
We've all been abused some way or other.
We must move on,
dwell on the positive.—
The main story was the Pope
and his visit;
offering friendship,
and—for the first time in decades
(ever, perhaps?)—relationship
... a meeting at least.

Done in face of politics; of history
(made by others, but compromising
all of us, all descending from that past).
And this story was lost.

All I can recall, now,

Perceptions

is what I have stated;
'though I remember,
and can summon up, what I saw;
darkness with light, in a cave perhaps?

The light, struggling
to show its quality,
to show its strength over evil,
its force in the face of the trivial
gossip,
produced by the media's susceptibility
to blame;

which, by its rooting out of pain,
makes healing ever more distant,
makes it recede
into a morass of court cases, compensation,
and the crime of ever more bitter
memories.

Move on!
See the good!
Help the good
to be good once more!

The Pope visited Israel in May 2009.

Perceptions

Passengers

England!—between culture and culture—
with the smell of morning coffee and breakfast eggs,
and the shadows of white clouds,
darkening green fields, red earth; wide rivers,
obscurely ending by neat squares of rice,
palm-trees, and pineapples, a row of tiny farm-houses.

Temporarily freed
from activity, responsibility, and duty,
it is easy to reflect
on the posture of national writers—
flown in, to share
their views, their work, their country,
with some other natives, anywhere.

With such a brief, why should they listen
to what others say? Living by asserting
their own right to a voice, why should they
be practised
in seeing things
from another's—The Other's—point of view?

Creative Writing Workshop, with visiting writers from the UK, held in South-East Asia.

International Relations

Country lanes are the same everywhere
in this modern world;
big enough for a tractor, truck or single car.
And farmers everywhere need
separation of this and that: bulls from cows
except in due season; sheep from clover always
(as Hardy taught his readers);
shelter from the sun, trees to break
the wind (no jokes please) and covers to
keep the straw at least somewhat dry
in case it rains before we get it in.

But farmers are conservative,
resisting novelty, strangers, in-comers.

If farmers meet farmers, though
—at farmers' conventions, world congresses—
I guess they acknowledge their sameness.

— Should we ask farmers, then,
to make friends for us with the rest
of the world?

September 2009

Perceptions

One Species

Perceptions

Cats

Experiment : to stare in the eyes of the black jaguar in the Hong Kong Botanic Gardens.

Was Blake right
when he talked of tigers' eyes as bright?
Was Kipling right,
when he claimed,
no animal
can meet the gaze of man,
steadily, unafraid?

Kipling's wolf-child,
Mowgli,
looks up, innocently,
at the big beasts,
making them turn their heads,
uneasy and ashamed.

An adolescent, Mowgli knew his power,
used it deliberately,
to gain a point
in the council of the jungle,
or to deflect brute attack on him,
the weakest of the beasts.

But I have looked in the eyes of big cats too.

They are not bright.

They burn with intelligence
of neither man, nor brute.

They don't slightly turn aside

Perceptions

their heads; but still they will not meet my gaze.
This happens ...

The tiger's head directly faces mine.
I place myself before his eyes.
I try to intercept
what consciousness is there,
behind the eyes: in vain.

What does he focus on?

He does <u>not</u> ... see,
but feign he does not see, me.
Simply there is something else
on which it seems his gaze alights.
Nor does he see through me.
—I do not think he consciously
decides to cut me (as a social lion might).—

Something else preoccupies his soul.

There is nothing the other side of me,
or in the real distance beyond;
there is nothing substantial there,
on which his darkness rests.

Perhaps his eyes are full of forests—
leaves and dark lianas
climbing up and round,
and butterflies
with decisive indecision,
flitting round—
reflected there, from times when,
as a cub, he gambolled free.

Perceptions

But if they are,
these past experiences
leave no impression
on his mind.

Of course, tigers have a low IQ!
Not as high as 5 or 10....
Of non-ape beasts, pigs are the most intelligent;
And even they score a mere 18.

This tiger would not comprehend
the insolent defiance of a man.
He could not feel uncomfortable
if a man gazed in his eyes.
For he would not see, not register the event.

Indeed he's forged on Blakean anvil by a hand divine,
set going by the divine clockmaker
to crash and tear and snarl and stink
in a damp darkness, occasionally riven by the light.

Cats are another matter.
Domesticated over time themselves,
they know this domestic creature, man.
They have learnt his desire
for undeserved authority
and pander (panda) to it just so far.

They gaze back
when a man stares hard into their eyes;
then turn their look away, after a while.

Man thinks his greatly-loved
companion cat
pretends this game bores him.
Really, he thinks,
his cat acknowledges

his own authority
by this veer in gaze.—
Each man thinks himself
the grown Mowgli,
strong and brave.

In fact, domesticated cats
merely indulge their man.

For in their other actions,
cats all show the low opinion
that they hold of him;

behave to him—
not intimately,
as towards other cats—
but treat him as an inanimate thing;
a being of no consequence,
except as a something
to rub against
to satisfy some itch.

Tigers and cats—
caged in a zoo,
or in our homes—
all know
how to put us
in our conceptual place!

Perceptions

Variety

A ring-tailed lemur baby, kitten-tiny,
clings flat to mother's back;
briefly separates; then clings to her underside.

An adult pulls the tail of another, inviting play.
Another bounds about a bit, looks around a bit.

One sits alone; three sit huddled. The bounder
joins them.
Another grooms not far away.

The black and white ruffed lemurs, said rarely
to descend to the ground, have broken their habit.

The rat-like agouti caresses its own tail,
as if it were its young, chirps like a bird,
and is alert to visiting outsiders ... birds and humans.

Sleek golden-lion tamarins
roll in paired balls on the concrete,
wrestle, and swing on the trees.

Then a riot of noise bursts out from a neighbour.
Their small faces look out, watchful, alert, concerned.

Buff-cheeked gibbons practice their brachination.
But —What a pity!—it is not the right time to hear
the male and female calls in song-like duet.

People circumambulate
as on a greened cruise-ship,
walking in pairs or jogging.
Some do tai-chi; others practice
with an aluminium sword.

Perceptions

Some walk, slapping their hands;
others slap their legs. ... All very healthy
and self-determined.

Black and white ruffed lemurs make
loud outbursts to mark their territory:
one starts, and another takes up, the calls,
circling the cage;
loud deep calls roar; but some lighter notes too.
"Aah," a high voice sings out repeatedly,
with no variety. "Aah," "Aah," "Aah".

The sloths, as one would expect, are being slothful.

The chelonia[1] collection of turtles, tortoises, and red-
eared sliders[2] has temporarily collected itself elsewhere.

The white-faced saki, with their rare
colour dichromatism,[3] are beginning to stir.

A siamang gibbon[4] twiddles her thumbs,
carefully examining her palms.

The male orangutan still
lumbers and slumbers under his sack-cloth.

A female sits on her hands, clasped,
breathing deeply, as if meditating or praying.

What can we learn from these behaviours,
social, individual?—

That mammalian life, in its many forms,
is similar?

that we all live in some form of cage?

Perceptions

Can we not all stick together? ...
help them—their families in the wild—to survive;
and so learn that survival has to be worked at?

Botanic Gardens, Hong Kong, September 2009.

An Almost Human Voice

An almost human voice called and called
a name.

What delight ... ungainly two-footed rush
of flying things there was
when the Keeper came!

—company ... boredom relieved ... more food—
"Ah Siu, Ah Siu!"

Red buckets, blue bowls,
tin bowl put in a tree.

Not alarm, not territorial defense,
as I supposed, at first.

"Chou-san" ("Good-morning"), she said
to the parrots, cranes, hoopoes;

blue-footed among parrots,
calling, calling, "Ah Siu!"—her name.

Hong Kong, 15 September 2009

Perceptions

Intimates

The strip of grass,
dividing the airport road,
had enough to offer a meal to a cow;

—and there was the cow, grazing;

and at her side, squatting down
intimately and familiarly,
was her owner,
his stick across his knees,
close to her,
looking at her,
talking to her:

"Now, Daisy,
you fill yourself up; you make a good meal.
I'll just squat here,
next to you,
keeping you company,
till you're done."

It was exciting to see
such familiarity
between man and beast;
the good relations we ought to have;
which we remember from our childhoods past
—or the childhoods we should have had, but never did—
and that our futures never can retrieve.

And we traveling people, flying here and there,
in and out of countries,
watching news on television
of the species, that are dangerously close to death,

Perceptions

Is there anything we do, but regret?

Will we change one iota of what we do,
day by day, to mitigate the causes,
accumulating towards such a loss?

"As flies to wanton boys are we to the gods;
They kill us for their sport." So Shakespeare wrote.

The human species acts thus too.

Maybe we cannot escape our own extinction
in due course.—"Those whom the gods
wish to destroy, they first make mad."—

But until then, let us act like gods
ourselves; and save those species that we can.

On the way from Mother Teresa Airport to the centre of Tirana, Albania, 17 October 2010.

Perceptions

Perceptions

Staring

Perceptions

Don't Stare!

"Don't stare at people!"
my Mother said,
and I observed this lesson
well; until,
one day, in downtown Lagos,
I saw,
passing by
on the opposite side
of the road,
the tallest, largest,
most imposing
man I had ever seen,
gowned in flowing robes,
swiftly walking in a measured way.

And—as a reflex—my head swivelled to stare at him,
all lessons forgot.

Seen 1968-1970, written 2009.

Lion's Pride

Waiting yourself,
you ask *us* to wait
and no-one minds.

You
are in your element,
dispensing
distant love to ladies
—however briefly—
lonely,
lunching alone,
in twos and threes,
without their
mates.

—Leo,
the politely posturing,
ever so slightly
—but politely—
presuming,
sincerely
caring
Maitre D'.

October 2005

Perceptions

Cross-culturally-clothed

Japanese lady, your straight back
adorns your square-shouldered jacket in smart silk,
western-style.

2008

"In a handbag?!"

> —Lady Bracknell, in Oscar Wilde's play,
> *The Importance of being Ernest*

It's not only women who
covet bags and bags and bags—
which Freud saw
as symbols for the womb;
pairing pencils, pens and obelisks,
his phallic symbols.—

Bags symbolize our hopes.

They are ready to
carry whatever we want,
whatever we desire.

Having a bag is
the first step to
having everything we want.

2009

Free Daily Newspaper

His eyes and face showed
how glad he was
to possess
even a newspaper
that he could not read.

Perhaps, for him
it represented
another blanket
against the coming cold.

December 2010

Perceptions

Flower Show, 2009

The human flowers—
so much more beautiful
than what they've come to see!

Groups of old people
willingly keep formation at first,
but soon dare to grasp back
individuality,
which even the massed pansies,
marigolds and petunias have,
if you look closely.

Children willingly tag along.

A field day for photographers, of course;
but even we are forced to select,
discriminate.—Too much plenitude,
beauty, creativity—life—to
internalize *all* in our cameras,
or even our thoughts.

The challenged are here in droves.

If they look closely at the flowers,
there is comfort there.—Difficult to find
perfect specimens!—All are faded,
wilting, damaged to a degree. Only
taken together, do they *seem* perfect.

Totalitarian states, doubtless
See things the same way.

Hong Kong Flower Show, Victoria Park, Hong Kong Island, 2009

Aesthetic Taste

The sparrow, pausing, head inclined,
holds mimosa in his beak.

The hobo lying on the city street, with crude vase near,
holds a red rose in his gaze.

The small girl holds her full skirt out, self-pleased.

The large exotics draw the passing eye
of older members visiting their club—
lilies of the field that toil not, neither
do they spin;
      whose beauty
justifies itself and us for loving it.

24 May 2010

Perceptions

Embodiment

Gravely, with sonorous bold
discords, they reveal
the music
that stained-glass window saints
and faded fresco angels made
before God, long centuries ago;
the sudden brief sweet
melody equally pleasing
to His ears.

The pace increases—excited,
running away.—God's
foot surely tapped too.

Then the sparkling finale!

The performance achieved,
angels and saints possess
their hearers' souls.

Artist adherents, inspired,
give the heard music
colour and form,
showing us sounds
otherwise silenced by time,
change,
and lack of constancy.

Matta-Rouch Trio (France), concert at the Sports Centre, Ordino, Principat d'Andorra (Principality of Andorra), Saturday, 8 August 2009, as part of the Eleventh Gathering of Bagpipers at Ordino.

The Blessèd Ones

Some cultures call them the blessèd ones;
but some might think them cursed:
with their unusual features, gait and awkward manners.

At mass, one man, receiving the host,
thanked the priest, once, twice, three times,
awkward, pleased.

After mass, an Irish trio plays a gig;
which some of us enjoy, pay attention to.

But for the same simple man,
there were other interests.
He sees a sweet white dog,
comfy on its master's lap,
goes near it; without touching,
conveys he likes it;
and the dog responds, leans out and sniffs.

He would like to touch it, pet it; almost
does so, but can't quite dare.
Will the dog accept him? Or is
he beyond the pale of dogs as well as men?

Yet what comfort a friendly
lick would give! I wish the dog's master
would see the man, understand his case,
encourage him to pet it,
cajole him to be a little brave!

Nearby, two men—pals for the holiday, at least—take
photos of each other.
      —*Ordino, August 2010*

Perceptions

Kindness

Every country has them:
mothers begging with a child.

The young woman sat on the ground,
her fair-haired toddler sitting
between her stretched-out legs.

A man had stopped in front of her,
and was speaking to her; kindly
questioning her situation. She
was leaning forward, eagerly answering.

Maybe she said, "There's only me, and I don't have
enough to feed her, clothe her, school her."

And he listened kindly, drawing a wallet out
of his pocket, as he listened and questioned.

Women like that, I've seen before, many of them:
not all as pretty, or young, or apparently so honestly
engaging with a questioning passer-by;

But what I've never seen before is
a passer-by like this, not putting down a coin
and walking past; but so kindly
stopping, asking, looking at the
face of her who begged for alms;
taking time to hear and show his feeling
for her plight; taking out his wallet, not hurrying by.

I don't think he would later give
her a coupon for a soup kitchen
where a Bible or Koran would be
gently—or not so gently, perhaps—offered her.

Perceptions

I feel sure he was a private person,
acting out of his own heart's
kindness and good-will.

So could we all do, if not made cynical
by those common professional beggars,
whom we see every day, instructed
by triads,
who know how to play on our sympathy.

Tirana, Albania, 18 October 2010

Perceptions

"An Action Produces an Equal and Equivalent Reaction"? (*Newton's Third Law*)

All I did was smile and greet you politely—
"Good Morning!"—as you sat by yourself
in your peasant's black trousers and jacket,
on a country bench, by a high wall in the shade,
as I walked with a small group, down a cobbled
path, to the museum of ethnography
in Krujë, close by the castle.

What less could one do, trooping past you—
presumably on your home turf—but see you,
show you one saw you, acknowledge
your prior rights?

But you—so generously and kindly
(respectfully? —no, not that word—lovingly, almost)
rose to your feet
and bowed deeply,
with your right hand on your heart.

Albania, 22 October 2010

Yoked

Twisted old gent, with white hair,
slowly descending
make-shift steps on a slope,
carrying a yoke of rusty, twisted, old metal....

Will the end of his adventure be
only two pails of warm milk?

Albania, 23 October 2010

Widespread

Does machismo really mean
spreading your legs wide
in the subway,
and occupying two seats?

23 December 2010

Perceptions

Legs

Lying prone on the walkway,
your stump and your shoe-clad prosthetic beside your
one good leg,
looking up at the other legs going past,

what do you think?— It's a way of life, a job?

Yes, your parents maimed you
to secure you livelihood.

Other parents
thought of a different way for their sons,
"Study! Pass exams!"

Some emotions, some freedom of movement, of
choice—for them—were lopped off, too....

2011

Construction, Destruction

An age-old scene:
the boat, the nets,
two people.

Not far away...
a more modern sight:
green nets—shrouds for
new buildings—
slightly contain the falling shards
of construction,

that in due course will bring
destruction to the fish,
the nets, the boats, the people,
a way of life;

us people too.

6 May 2011

Perceptions

Passing On

Perceptions

Storage Space

Sick to death of that click click
click click click click click?
as your zip drive cheerfully
destroys the work of the past three years ...
three months ... three days?

Are you sick to death of that click?

... sick to death of the uphill battle
as successive blood clots,
caused by the failing
pump of her heart,
lodge in her brain and blow her mind,
bit by bit, away—
away from the deep veins, where
what was in her loving, desiring,
sad and angry
heart
had lodged,
incrementally,
life long—

she lies, not always patiently,
and waits.

Death click,[5] death rattle: still not quite the same.

March 2004

Choices

A long life has much to say for it;
one must select what to say. And
life itself—however long—is itself
a selection from what might
have been done. You chose, it seems,
to serve other men's words and meanings—
in libraries, on a publisher's then editor's
desk, as speech-writer and breaker of codes.

And the place where you chose to live—somewhat
predetermined by your place of birth—
Wuhan, Hubei, in China (a missionary's son)—
also, as it seems, signposted
the areas for your life-time's work
(Asia and Asian Studies mainly)—
necessarily excluded—or at least
diminished—other subjects that you might equally
have beamed your search-light on.

We have benefited from these choices;
also from your courtesy, concern
and conscientiousness, and yes,
from your curiosity and cushioning too.

You persisted in teasing-out
other men's meanings. Doubtless
you knew your own meanings too.
Is there anyone left who will unpick
your puzzle for us all to read,
and then, know you better than we did?

2010

Perceptions

Perceptions

Reading On and In

Perceptions

Dangerous Mis-Communication

If the boat sank and the waters rose,
would someone die
if they read,
on the safety notice in front of them,
"Lift Jacket under seat",
and not, "Life Jacket under seat"—
which, of course, is what
it means?

November, 2006

Truer Than it Seems

"Beware of discarded love!"—
An odd notice, I thought.

Looking closer, I read more accurately,
"Beware of dengue fever!"

Well...

The pain of dengue, I have heard,
feels like
someone
has taken a hammer
to every bone.

A discarded lover
suffers the same way,

I am sure.
17 July 2010

Eden Marriage Registry

Walking towards Macau Ferry Terminal,
something caught my eye:
"Eden Marriage Registry".

Why did it tug so at my sub-conscious?...
call for selective attention,
from among the many richly denotative objects
in this urban—but not urbane—harbour location;
where China steamers have come and gone
for a century and more,
bringing east and west into touch?

Eden? The person who chose the name
had obviously heard the phrase,
"Happy as in the Garden of Eden",
and thought "Eden" a good name
for a place, where that beginning of all happiness—
marriage with the one we love—is formalized.

But what about the apple of desire,
the temptation of the serpent?
The ambition of Eve? The reluctant obedience
of her man, Adam, to her advice?
And the consequences!—
Banishment from Eden and the couple's loss
of previous, immortal status?

Is this really
what we want
the happy pair to bear in mind,
as they seal their fate;
then set out perhaps
for the gambling saloon,
as the best way they can find

Perceptions

to mark the biggest gamble of their lives?

Yes, small knowledge is dangerous.

Increasingly,
cross-culturality
gives occasion
to demonstrate that fact.

5 December 2009

Suspension Cables

Two triangles,
Two peacocks' tails,
Two herrings' bones:[6]

Distant, bridge cables
strike the eye unaware,
interrogating the mind,
as the surprised eye sees
three sets as two.

23 December 2010

Persuasion

Aeroflot—presumably proud
of its safety standards—

has spent money on an ad,
showing a pilot, in-flight,

busy,

tightening
a screw to the ceiling of his plane.

I am not persuaded to travel by this.
Are you?

December 2010

Perceptions

Times and Occasions

Eve of New Year's Eve

The golden wine
of a Chopin nocturne
and the bright balloons
of his Polonaise
fill the evening space
with quiet, meant emotion.

2006, 20 April 2008

Middle Age

Middle age is when new fashions are old
and your spouse needs to buy you
a business, or an apartment—or even both—
to give you anything new.

Edited from notes, 2006

Christmas Party

Christmas is Dylan Thomas,
"A Child's Christmas in Wales",
and Eliot, T. S.—
"A cold coming we had of it"—
Laurie Lee, sparkling and crisp,
with bells and stars and frost…
but I've forgotten his words.

Who else?

"Lully, Lullay, thou little tiny child",
holly and mistletoe,
"Tannenbaum, O tannenbaum",
and only very recently,
the reindeer Randolph,
and his red, red nose.

Hong Kong Writers' Circle Christmas party, 4 December 2009.

Perceptions

Writers' Party

There was a young man from Hong Kong
whose—sentences—were extraordin'r'y long.

But he cut them quite short.

He now finds life fraught.

That truncated young man from Hong Kong.

Lawrence Gray's 56th birthday / HK Writers' Circle Christmas Party, 6 December 2008

Penguin Party

There was a young bird
who found <u>life</u> quite absurd.
But … after turning the sheets of a Penguin,
she felt considerably sanguine,
And—yes!—satisfyingly stirred.

Written at a party to celebrate seventy years of Penguin Books, held at Bookazine's Jardine House basement store in November 2005. Read carefully, this does follow classical limerick rules: that is, a rhyme scheme of aabba and a stress count of 3,3,2,2,3.

Lessons from the Plants, 1.

Lacking coherence and a sense of place,
when seeds, they are scattered close together;

when seedlings of a certain age and stature,
planted out;

when in the full bloom
of youthful maturity,
taken into society;

and the day the best
begins to seem past,

removed.

Lessons from the Plants, 2.

As long as you're pretty, young
and fresh, you can stay where you are.
Once faded, wilting or dead,
up you come!

Perceptions

Meetings and Memories

Perceptions

Friends

The greasy-spoon cook smiled at me,
commenting to his mates.
Then he reached inside his stained shirt,
to show
dangling ornaments,
"Buddhism," he said.

Understanding what he meant,
I reached inside my own upper garment
—probably slightly more elegant—
to show
my single flash-drive.
"Computer," I said.

Some delay in comprehension occurred.
"Computer," I said again.
"Memory.
"Many things in here."

He pretended at least to understand.
"Computer!" he exclaimed,
and pretended pleasure
at this revelation.

But we were still new friends.

Maxim's restaurant, City Hall High Block, Hong Kong Island, 20 March 2009.

Daylight

As daylight breaks
and the world lightens,
the clouds darken.

In time,
light brightens 'round their edges.

So, virtue, energy, ability,
kindness
highlight their reverse;

and when the right
circumstances
prevail,

nibble away at their edges.

Seen from Hotel Tryp Barcelona Aeropuerto, 2009.

Perceptions

Memory

In 1931,
Kerd came to Hawaii,
an eleven-years' boy;

saw four girls dance the hula,
remembered their names;
returned as an adult.

The girls were gone,
but the same palm trees
framed the same show.

Honolulu museum, July 2010.

I Touched the Wall

I touched the wall, my point of turn-
around, and asked myself,
Will this feel of dappled render
come in time to be the feel for me
of all accomplishment?—Let me
experiment...
      ... use this scientific goal
to support
this daily morning walk;
the other daily delights;
and the self-argument—Walking is working too!—
that we must use,
to persuade ourselves away
from instant access to our world of words
on every awakening,

ensuring I enjoy the other walkers,

who—more knowledgeably, perhaps—
with careful exaggeration swing
their arms,
but whose shorter legs still mean
they walk more slowly through the park;
some halting
 to beat their stomachs for purposes unknown;
some—themselves seemingly uncertain
of their purpose—who slightly call to mind
Shakespeare's schoolboy,
creeping unwillingly to school;
        some—aging
and sideways bent—determinèdly circle
the grouped palm-trees and laboriously
raise an arm to greet me, as do
the school night-watchmen, now used to me

Perceptions

and my own cheerful wave of hand to them.

The dogs are another matter. Some know
their purposes are publicly to perform
private acts efficiently, quickly and as copiously as possible;
know their companions, slightly embarrassed,
secretly dislike the task of walking them,
making it palatable by texting friends, reading the paper,
and generally "walking the dog" as little as they can.

But others happily take their humans for a walk,
unleashed illegally; and I hold back
from greeting them, unwilling either to
seduce or be snapped at, to be sniffed too
intimately—among strangers, after all!

But let us continue. ...

Here is the tiny knot garden,
its sturdy tall shrubs enlivened by delicate flowers.

The China Sea.... A single small boat pulls in its nets,
son helping his mother perhaps, to continue
this dying occupation,
until, hakka hat put aside,
she rows to another shore
and he seeks work on land.

More distant, a boat sits, with its four
elongated, jointed, crustacean legs
awaiting its bigger catch.

In the distance, Hong Kong and Kowloon hills
and other heights are seen through a haze that
Turner would have liked to paint. (Another day,
a rising sun turns ones eyes away.)

Perceptions

To the right, absent egrets on a single tree
and close shore line....

—The other day, something
had disturbed them. They had risen up
and now wheeled around; and
it was interesting to see the pattern
of their reattachment to the land;
some quickly crowded the tree; some took
the opportunity to take a break
from the crowd, and stayed relatively long away.
In fact, some took so long I resumed my walk:
No time to observe them further.

Low tide and a little sandy beach beneath
the rubber tires, broken witches' hat and other
mysteries of modern use, now disused, diseased,
and awaiting a small boy or stranded sea-farer
to provide new use and sense of purpose ...

which we all need—objects, birds, dogs, people—
to feel whole, wholesome and free of nothingness.

Discovery Bay, Hong Kong
27 September 2010

Perceptions

Pride

Bull-frogs in the drain,
are proud in the echo-chamber
we have given them.

23 December 2010

On Bus Number Eleven

Ugly buildings have the beauty
of the work that has been done in them,
the holy, honest, daily effort to provide
food, shelter, education—decency
for themselves, their families...

This—what takes place within—beautifies
old shabby buildings in—maybe—despised parts of town,
as much as loving thoughts make a plain face glow.

30 January 2011

Water

The gardener drew a magic circle of water-drops
around him and her, sitting, reading their papers,
staring at their inner thoughts.

But me he slightly dampened,
sprinkling bag and baggage
with precious drops,
wanting to reach through me to the thirsty plants beyond.

This happened today.

And the message was?

When someone appears
bringing freshness to life,
remove obstructions,
be receptive,
let the drops of novelty—however inconvenient—
touch you. Receive the message
and grow from its touch!

2011

Perceptions

Individualist / Social Critic

It was a strange thing to see on a beach,
This Snowman,
with his purple scarf,
pipe, and shell (not coal-black) eyes.

It was not a long wait, to
see him melt,
the packed snow pack up,
the heat
penetrate his absent bones.

...

Before the judge could come,
he had shut up shop
and gone.

Written as follow-up to a workshop led by Thad Rutkowski at Discovery Bay, Lantau Island, Hong Kong, 18 April 2011. Task. Write a piece using the following words in the order given: "Beach, snowman, purple, wait, pack, penetrate, judge, shop".

The Senses of Morning

Light under meeting trees
and the early morning empty garden seat
facing another.

Paired seats facing the China Sea.

Seats at the side of tennis courts.

The pleasure of birds.

The pattern of the wrought iron fence—

so we see only it;
no distant view;

—locking our sight, which dwells on
the patterned tiles, re-patterned by
shadow from sunlit fences
and the leaves that grow
and cling to them.

The sentinels of umbrellas
by the pool.

The school staff
under their canopy of metal tubes and glass—
which one tries to see
as a conservatory of sorts—
to calm the impact
of this shocking stark city idiom,
sitting in this carefully composed park.

And the other senses?—

Perceptions

Sound ... birds,
lapping waves, busy fountain.

Smell ... mainly grass;
until we reach a group of persons
—Walkers? Workers?—
not yet washed.

Touch ... pebbled paths.

Perception?
... All of this.

Discovery Bay, Lantau Island, Hong Kong, 2011

Perceptions

Perceptions

Perceptions

Notes

[1] The super-order uniting turtles, tortoises and terrapins. (Wikipedia.org) Some of these are on the brink of extinction, although protected by law.
[2] Semi-aquatic turtles. (Wikipedia.org)
[3] "The difference between the sexes is considerable. Adult males are black, with the striking white face. The females are brownish-grey and have only a narrow white stripe on the face between the inner eye and mouth. Colour differences like this between the sexes are termed 'sexual dichromatism'." (Bristol (UK) Zoo website, <www.bristolzoo.org.uk/whitefaced-saki>, seen 15 June 2011.)
4 "The siamang is the largest and darkest species of gibbon. Siamangs are rare, small, slender, long-armed, tree-dwelling (lesser) apes. These very acrobatic primates live in southeast Asia. Siamangs are arboreal; they spend most of their lives in trees. Because they are so dextrous while moving in the trees, almost no predators can catch them. The siamang is one of nine species of gibbons. The siamang is the largest, darkest, and noisiest species of gibbon. Because of the rapid deforestation of their habitats, gibbons are an endangered species." (Enchanted Learning website, <www.enchantedlearning.com/subjects/apes/siamang>, seen 15 June 2011)
[5] "Click to death": jargon for the signal that a zip-disk is going to wipe itself out.
[6] I did toy with the question of whether it should be "two herring bones" or "two herring's bones"; but decided that the latter suited the meaning better.

Perceptions

THE INTERNATIONAL PROVERSE POETRY PRIZE (SINGLE POEMS)

An annual international Proverse Poetry Prize (for single poems) was established in 2016. The international Proverse Poetry Prize is open to all who are at least eighteen years old whatever their residence, nationality or citizenship.

Single poems, submitted in English, are invited on (a) any subject or theme, chosen by the writer OR (b) on a subject or theme selected by the organizers each year.

Poems may be in any form, style or genre. Each poem should be no more than 30 lines.

Entries should previously be unpublished in any way (except in the case of unpublished translations into English of the entrant's own work already published in another language, providing the entrant holds the copyright).

In 2016, cash prizes were offered as follows:
1st prize; USD100.00; 2nd prize: USD45.00;
3rd prizes (up to four winners): USD20.00.

KEY DATES FOR THE PROVERSE POETRY PRIZE IN 2017 ONWARDS
(subject to confirmation and/or change)

Receipt of entered work, entry forms and entry fees	7 May to 14 July of the year of entry
Announcement of Winners	Before April of the year following the year of entry
Cash Awards Made	At the same time as publication of the winning poems (whether in the Proverse newsletter or website, or in an anthology)
Publication of an anthology of winning and other selected entries	Contingent on the quality of entries in any year

The above information is for guidance only. More information, updated from time to time, is available on the Proverse website: proversepublishing.com

POETRY AND POETRY COLLECTIONS
Published by Proverse Hong Kong

Astra and Sebastian, by L.W. Illsley. 2011.
Chasing light, by Patricia Glinton Meicholas. 2013.
China suite and other poems, by Gillian Bickley. 2009.
For the record and other poems of Hong Kong,
 by Gillian Bickley. 2003.
Frida Kahlo's Cry and Other Poems,
 by Laura Solomon. 2015.
Home, away, elsewhere, by Vaughan Rapatahana. 2011.
Immortelle and bhandaaraa poems,
 by Lelawattee Manoo-Rahming. 2011.
In vitro, by Laura Solomon. 2nd ed. 2014.
Irreverent Poems for Pretentious People,
 by Henrik Hoeg. 2016.
Moving house and other poems from Hong Kong,
 by Gillian Bickley. 2005.
Of Leaves & Ashes, by Patty Ho. 2016.
Of symbols misused, by Mary-Jane Newton. 2011.
Painting the borrowed house: poems,
 by Kate Rogers. 2008.
Perceptions, by Gillian Bickley. 2012.
Rain on the pacific coast, by Elbert Siu Ping Lee. 2013.
refrain, by Jason S. Polley. 2010.
Shadow play, by James Norcliffe. 2012.
Shadows in Deferment, by Birgit Bunzel Linder. 2013.
Shifting Sands, by Deepa Vanjani. 2016.
Sightings: a collection of poetry, with an essay, 'communicating poems', by Gillian Bickley. 2007.
Smoked pearl: poems of Hong Kong and beyond,
 by Akin Jeje (Akinsola Olufemi Jeje). 2010.
The Burning Lake, by Jonathan Locke Hart. 2016.
The Layers Between (Essays and Poems),
 by Celia Claase. 2015.
Unlocking, by Mary-Jane Newton. March 2014.
Wonder, lust & itchy feet, by Sally Dellow. 2011.

Perceptions

FIND OUT MORE ABOUT OUR AUTHORS BOOKS, EVENTS AND LITERARY PRIZES

Visit our website:
http://www.proversepublishing.com

Visit our distributor's website: <www.chineseupress.com>

Follow us on Twitter
Follow news and conversation: twitter.com/proversebooks>
OR
Copy and paste the following to your browser window and follow the instructions:
https://twitter.com/#!/ProverseBooks
"Like" us on www.facebook.com/ProversePress

Request our free E-Newsletter
Send your request to info@proversepublishing.com.

Availability
Most titles are available in Hong Kong and world-wide
from our Hong Kong based Distributor,
The Chinese University of Hong Kong Press,
The Chinese University of Hong Kong, Shatin, NT,
Hong Kong SAR, China.
Email: cup-bus@cuhk.edu.hk
Website: <www.chineseupress.com>.
All titles are available from Proverse Hong Kong
http://www.proversepublishing.com
and the Proverse Hong Kong UK-based Distributor.

We have **stock-holding retailers** in Hong Kong,
Singapore (Select Books),
Canada (Elizabeth Campbell Books),
Andorra (Llibreria La Puça, La Llibreria).
Orders can be made from bookshops
in the UK and elsewhere.

Ebooks
Most of our titles are available also as Ebooks.